AF244038

EMBERS

 FriesenPress

One Printers Way
Altona, MB R0G 0B0
Canada

www.friesenpress.com

Copyright © 2024 by Howard Giskin
First Edition — 2024

All rights reserved.

No part of this publication may be reproduced in any form, or by any means, electronic or mechanical, including photocopying, recording, or any information browsing, storage, or retrieval system, without permission in writing from FriesenPress.

ISBN
978-1-03-830537-4 (Hardcover)
978-1-03-830536-7 (Paperback)
978-1-03-830538-1 (eBook)

1. POETRY, SUBJECTS & THEMES, PLACES

Distributed to the trade by The Ingram Book Company

EMBERS

HOWARD GISKIN

Contents

* * * * *

Poetry comes closest to expressing emotions, thoughts, and vague (though sometimes intense) perceptions that struggle to find language suitable to their subtle complexity. Like music or dance, poetry aims to embody realities that are beyond language. In this sense, poetry is language struggling to transcend itself. The poems in this collection are my attempts to express sentiments that seemed best said in the compressed form of verse—a sort of mental archeology, or perhaps therapy. Yet, in the end, it is for the reader to judge ... as words are no more the property of the writer than the air we breathe.

* * * * *

Carpe Diem

French kiss the here and now. Say no to promises of
rewards or punishments, of an afterlife ... of heaven. Line up and
buy a ticket.

There must have been a time when spirit knew no way but
one, like Zen wisdom telling us to see the world in a drop
of water, or sitting in the clouds with our feet deep in the moist
earth.

To know there is no one, no place, no up, and no down, and yet
"expect not long to hold thy breath/For heart of oak thou seest cut
off by Death."[1]

Ah yes ... Ah yes.

Evanescence

Used to describe an aspect of Japanese classical poetry,
I love this word for its subtlety, finesse, and
　　fine-fingered gossamer-smooth
molten caress … as if all of life is more than we can bear,
like smoke rising from a blacksmith's forge in a clang of senses,
and sweet-burning autumn sedge.

I love this word, and all it contains: its expanse, depth, and taste;
its soft spring grasses, mountain breezes, velvet meadows, and
translucent woven dewdrops. For fleeting gifts whose presence
tease with subtle beauty seasoned with loss, tears for antiquity,
ebbed in the creased folds of time.

For supple, slender leaves, awakened as I imperceptibly age,
frost gathering on my crown, delighting my senses, phantasms
in shadows flowing, ever moving, fallen, mirrored, concealing
beauty at last to keep by midsummer its unforgotten song;
whisper of wild, short-lived summer buds, invisible almost.

I am born and die in the longing rustle of fading leaves, disconsolate
in nights abandoned, fragile seasons grown old, perhaps because
autumn mists have ever reached and scattered melancholy hues.
How we will miss the soft white clouds, dyed in human frailty
to suit desire's lingering whims and love's regrets.

I love this word … its mountain winds and cherry petals, longing for
tears to mourn the damp valleys, hale passing from youth to age

that we may lose our way in savage remembrances of spring
cloudbursts vanishing, of rushing pines on mountain slopes, and
whispers of love alone
braided with
cut
reeds.

Todaiji

The train from Kyoto to Nara hums as we sit silently,
watching the Japanese—
some to work, others to visit a friend, a young mother with two
small children, a grizzled old man barely awake in a wheelchair—
as buildings speed by, jagged marks as time slows. For
we are interlopers and paid no attention.

The walk to the temple … a thousand years fallen away, hard to
grasp this moment drawing breath. But today is a holiday, so
crowds throng Japan's temples, dressed in colorful traditional
garb, while great Todaiji's deer mill about, begging for pellets
sold nearby.

Nara's Great Eastern Temple, with its Sun Buddha centered in
a lotus flower, free from causes and conditions, the life force that
illuminates the universe. Buddha Vairocana, dusted by monks in
August. *Sunyata, sunyata*, emptiness, the Dharma, the nature of
being in the light of our endless wanderings, each lotus leaf a
separate universe.

In days of yore, Kukai, Nara's son, crossed the sea to Tang, whose
masters taught arcane doctrines from far-off India; hard to fathom
such things as happened thirteen hundred years ago, now mere
echoes of the past as a foreign land more distant than Himalayan
slopes.

As the founder of *Shingon* must have done, we walk round the
colossal bronze figure, darkened with age, right hand raised palm
outward in a gesture of peace, atop a platform flanked by towering
red-cedar columns, as majestic to me as the Buddha himself—

thick columns legend says were cut from forests in distant parts of the nation, forded hundreds of miles on rivers large and small.

I wonder at what we have become. For a moment, I see all as brother and sister, calm radiating from the giant bronze, yet even Shakyamuni could not stop warring clans, or the rage in men's hearts. Still, beauty survives somehow. Sweet incense rising. Families enjoying a spring outing. I intone a silent prayer.

Memento Mori

My two earliest memories have to do with death. I must
have been five years old when this happened, watching
television in a house I barely remember, only snippets
of our front lawn and driveway. This memory is perhaps
the first of my life: watching television when suddenly
a wall collapses, a hideous white skeleton appears
on the screen, and an electric wave of terror passes through
my body:

Death ... subterranean
terror summoned at five years old...
someone else's not my own.

A dank dungeon I cannot explain.
Scarecrow effigy, mocking image,
gaping empty eye holes, devoid of soul, as if to say, *"You, child,
will be this."*
Freud's *unheimlich,* yet death too has been
friend and companion, for knowing the truth as a child
has been a gift. I have lived with this key, this opening
of a spiritual door, discontented searcher, wanderer,
landlocked seafarer. A doubter I have been.

Strange second solitary image
from this place long ago, nearly forgotten,
of a neighbor girl my age (four or five) with an angelic
face who died at the age of six—a disease no child should
have sweeping her away as if she were no more than God's
afterthought, yet I remember none of this. Only that she

and I, as mischievous children and companions in crime,
climbed into my father's Pontiac in our beveled driveway;
releasing the handbrake, the car rolled down into the
street.

So, death has followed me, ominous specter (though
wise teacher) whose eerie call I knew younger than most,
for my doppelganger, a child of six, had died while
I had lived.

Growing Up Jewish

A seed partially germinated, Passover Seder at Aunt Lillian's in the
distant land of my childhood: Uncle Leon with his shock of wavy
snow-white hair; Cousin Alice with her strange
    paralysis, with whom I once
smoked pot at Yale New Haven hospital.
Son of Abram and Sarai, Jerusalem, Babylon, Granada,
Minsk, Cairo, and Damascus.
In March 1964, we gather around Aunt's
    table for a few moments while
ancestors come alive.

Fragments swirl, broken-maelstrom shards of recollection,
assembling as if by magic lantern, a beautiful jumble, but it was the
stories I secretly thirsted for, so rare in my
    family, like how Uncle Leon's
father, a stalwart village peasant at eighty-eight, died when he was
struck by a car as he worked in a parking garage in New Haven. We
were Jews, so we remembered, but forgetting reigned also.

One year older than I, Cousin Burt led us children
    in a game of Red Light / Green
Light in the long, narrow living room while an empty chair and cup
of sweet wine at the table waited for Elijah to lift our spirits, always
in need of lifting, for the prophet above all hates injustice.

Housatonic

River of youth, unceasing ripples draw me to hopeful years,
bringing nurturing rains, dampening for a New England summer's
idyl, beauty allied with sadness, for all good cares call to mind
bygone times.

Bittersweet in the eyes of dawn, by river's mossy shore,
foamy crests rise and fall, tiny ships lasting
     but a second. Delicious scent
of wet earth, delightful, then evening by campfire, healing waters
not seen, though heard—a lullaby almost.

Vortex cradled, I could believe in wandering spirits by your banks,
solitary in lonely wilds. Still there was comfort in your yielding
nature, absent intention of good, for death was there also, and life,
in roiling waters.

Rushing, polished stone, elusive fire arrow, but still there is time
for playful jags on carefree days revisited, recollection's fickle
dance forsaking decades, never more. Lazy piers cool shaded as
motorboats skim and skid, glistening in sultry August warm.

Silently watching under a generous canopy, pitted-wood colonial
house, so clearly I see the riverside antique, sentinel of muddy earth,
"beyond the mountain place," *usi-a-di-en-uk* Algonquian echo,
the summer waters of clapboard cottages sleeping.

Children play, now grown, wind-blown,
     though do not misunderstand,
for time has been kind despite memory's savage hand.

RACING

We would ride our bikes, a kind of
pilgrimage, down Dixwell Avenue to a
little shop no bigger than my parents'
living room with a large plate-glass
window, so you could see a raised
electric track for diminutive sports cars.
Oh, how we prized and cared for our
tiny race cars, primping them like
fighting cocks.
Electronic plungers
in hand, we would careen the oval track
like our lives depended upon it, strange
now to behold in memory.

The old man who ran the shop long gone,
the shop surely too, familiar musty scent
(we looked forward to this), acrid hint
of sparked metal from our cars' copper
contacts (we loved this too). Thin waft
of fine oil for axel and moving parts, bare
lightbulb hanging from cracked beige
ceiling like a forgotten winter pear.

We loved the place as only thirteen-year-olds
can. What happened to my pampered
race car I cannot recall, perhaps abandoned
in a shoebox when I left behind adolescent
things, thrown away during some move
or another. Or maybe, by some twist of

fate, it has survived, forgotten as the
exigencies of life grew like mushrooms
after a spring rain. Strange small emptiness,
emblem of youth, circles on a track
that led nowhere and everywhere,
ascending spiral,
prayer wheel...

We knew not,
wanting nothing.

Imagined Ancestors

What echoes of faces do we see in the faces
of those living?
Tiny photos of family,
perhaps led into forests and
fields to be shot and buried
in a mass grave.
The thing is, I
simply do not know,
a gaping hole that can't
be filled. Mother's father was from Vilnius;
he had a brother, for I have seen an old
photo, a haunting profile of two young men,
swarthy of skin,
not unhandsome.

If they had sisters, I do not know.
What their parents,
my great-grandparents, looked like,
I do not know either.

The Ponary massacre of Vilnius killed 70,000
Jews thirty years after my grandfather left Lithuania,
which perhaps he had little regret to leave.
My grandfather's grave,
I have visited,
Grandmother's too,
but they refuse to speak,
or do they?

Do I have the strength to listen?
And if they speak, what could they say

to one such as me, a child of fortunate circumstance?
Grandmother kept secrets, for we do not know
from where she came, only Poland,
somewhere near the German border.
She had twin brothers, though God only knows
what happened to them.

Everything is left to the imagination now,
the leave-taking of parents,
brothers, sisters, grandparents, friends,
cousins, the inevitably unkept vows,
yet still some gravitational force
calls me as witness to what I have neither
seen nor heard: Ellis Island, flesh
of my flesh, with hopeful eyes,
trepidation too, the mass grave and others like it,
silent yet howling, near a railway station,
in *Reichskommissariat Ostland.*

But then, as we know, life carries on,
a blessing as well as a curse, so I will
soon visit my grandparents' graves,
where grass grows green, and trees
stand watchful sentinel under amber skies.

The Dream

Descending flight after flight of white marble
      stairs in an Egyptian tomb,
deeper and deeper, while reports of Mother's
      decline drip day by day.
Not scary this, well lighted, no sepulcher, all clean and neat.

What does it mean, this strange spiral image
      lodged in my brain? Jacob's
Ladder in reverse, yet somehow calming,
      for I felt no fear, trembling,
nor loneliness.

I strangely remember this dream, so I conclude
      it to be the sort that folk wisdom
calls us to heed, a psychopomp come to
      teach me something. About
Mother dying and something beautiful and
      serene rising to the surface.

As it descends into the unknown, death not
      untoward is strangely welcome.
A beautiful vision even as I see it now in my mind's eye,
hovering, white as wafting snow.

Wool carefully washed, a blank page begging
      for forgiving words, hard
also for there is something unforgiving in
      the expanse of anonymous
time poised to erase our being and having been.

Steps I see now in their earthward climb, aware as I am of the dream
within a dream that gives life then takes it away, staircase winding,
in ambient light, soft ... almost loving.

While dying's homely mask becalms an alien
        land, Mother lies sleeping,
all ninety-eight of her years stacked dominos
        about to fall. Still, I cannot
yet cry, for the incomprehensible silently gives way.

Long ago, a kite fluttering in the summer
        breeze, young and strong and
full of assured purpose, a child of five or six
        standing by. I am that child
as years melt away.

Mother appears again young and caring and
        full of love for her growing
brood. And so, these stairs draw me down yet into the light, this
moving image so like a cavernous mine I once saw.

Where men sweated and lived and died, yet carved exquisite figures
of pink-hued salt a thousand feet deep,
        subterranean treasures to equal
any above.

Growing Old

It is a curious feeling, imperceptibly sliding from one thing I do not
understand to another opaque to my intellect, growth but also loss.

Things added and stripped away, confidence yet rising fear, playing
the long game but fretting over little things.

Mother at ninety-eight would say, "Oh, to be eighty again!"
for the old can be young while the young ancient. Nâbî says:

> In the garden of time and destiny, we have seen both
>   the autumn and the spring
> We have seen both the time of joy and the time
>   of sorrow[2]

And so, of what we have seen, for the wise say to choose with an
eye on the horizon, as I have tried in life's coiled seasons.

For indeed it is a curious feeling, this quiet voice that grows louder
with the years, recollection haunting as past moments surge.

Circling gulls at sunset above a dappled beach, crescent moon
low above the surf.

Nature is a temple where living pillars
Sometimes give birth to veiled words;
There one passes through forests of symbols
Which observe with familiar eyes.

BAUDELAIRE[3]

NATURE

Green to forget, strangely pleasing
to one's soul
smoldering below the skin.

So small as to be invisible, Emerson's
transparent eyeball, over
sequoia rough.

Fertile loam, cascading waters,
untamed,
luxurious, riotous, joyous, relentless.

Roiling such as we cannot see,
unending, only Whitman's "urge
and urge and urge."

Irrevocably other, nature's
fantastic cypher, Delphic magus,
in language strange.

Tarifa

Languages gone silent, dust and souls floating about
as we walked
narrow shaded lanes shielded from the Mediterranean sun.
Thirteen hundred years ago, Tarif ibn Malak, dark Berber
from the foothills of Atlas,
came ashore as voices
of the past bayed silently
in la Iglesia de San Mateo Apostól—

Their voices I could hear below the humming
of lovers gliding through shady lanes,
a church built on mosque
ruins, built on a Roman temple to Diana or some other
tangible god, a dream in its vastness,
small remnant of a name,
or a life, or a memory that died six hundred years ago,
in a strange unsteady script,
etched laboriously onto a piece of stone,
placed in the church.

Tarif, who gave his name unknowing
to this windy sea-swept place,
came with four vessels from Tangier in the year 710,
naming what he saw Green Island
for its verdant cape, Visigothic Hispania
in his sights.
The rest is history.

So, on our third day, we retraced Tarif's journey
backward on a hulking steel ferry,
southerly to Tangier, walking slanted

lanes where our warrior may
have passed, centuries
melting under African sun, grist now
for musty tomes, forgotten amid the sparkling
haze of balmy nights and glasses of wine.

But Tarif returned in scarcely a year,
commander under Tariq ibn Ziyad,
launching Islamic conquest of Iberia,
inscribed somehow all these things,
in the book of memory, time,
bravery, and cowardice. Inscribed also
in our flesh as we slept in a house of
tile and stone.

PATER

With each death there is a stopping of the river of becoming,
those remaining submerged in the deep of recollection, memories
plum blossoms on a spring morning. Fragments. We have gone
to a park somewhere with Father, my brother and I. We are five and
six and have gone swimming in a lake, shiny polished stones
to be touched, examined, and placed on a shelf.

Yet, oh how my view of Father continues to evolve, to ebb and flow,
for though he no longer lives, he lives still, eternal,
and I too own a bit of it, for we move closer to time's
bottomless well as the old ones pass.

It is the small things that matter: Father teaching me how to
write a check at sixteen, as I do now at sixty-six. He was
dutiful, reserved, occasionally angry, and hated incompetence in
his professional life, though he was forgiving
        of family. Now he moves
away from me, or I from him … his life, his
        presence, his being a thing
ever fading, this leave taking as in Homer's subterranean world
of shadows, vague and intangible, far from sun and soil, from
real to myth, gritty lineaments of flesh smoothed over to make
fable.

Father waves from a distance, features unclear.
Again then, images come rushing in, sluice opened,
for now, again,
I am five in Father's sea-green Pontiac somewhere in
Pennsylvania at night as we leave the hospital where my
mother will soon give birth to my sister.

A deer leaps,
and I slam into the metal dashboard.
So, back to the hospital for stitches and the
birth of my sister.
No pain do I feel, only the tap-tap of past
life reborn.

Hunting

Skeet rifles in hand, in a field of tall grass, we waited for a
clear shot. At ten, I was doubtful, though dutifully followed,
hearing for the first time that curious inner voice saying, *no.*
Do not ... Do not ... rather watch and learn.

But still I followed,
grass swaying in the cool fall air.
I was shown how to load a skeet rifle,
crack it open, slip the cherry-red skeet packet into the gun,
snap it closed, careful to point downward the barrel.

Then we waited
for movement in the sky or the grass.
Swept along, some tide pulling, I fired, hitting nothing,
shoulder jolted by the gun's power.
Oh, rue the day or year of such an invention,
progeny of sticks and stones, spears, bows and
arrows, some Adam first flinging a deadly piece, bludgeoning
with sharp rock, jabbing with ragged stick.

And so, for one hour, we fingered our guns.
I fired again, signal crack and sweet
gunpowder scent (not unpleasant) in the autumn beauty of
the place, browning grasses, and pleasant whiff of dry earth,
yet still how strange this all is, for hunters argue killing is ancestral,
from remotest times.

And so, I wonder at the ancient who refused
to hunt when it was a matter of survival, ignominy of one who
would not kill thirty-thousand years ago, forgotten pacifist

among those who depended for survival on the great and noble
hunt, prowess of men (and women).

Now, we who eat the flesh of animals
(myself included)
are shamefully separated from the killing.
I never again fired a gun, nor even touched one
(though perhaps in a museum once).

So, when we'd emptied our barrels
and headed back, rifles aimed earthward,
I felt relief. Father and I were neither
of us hunters—nor would ever be—no complex reasoning
needed, precocious articles nor tomes to read, deeper and
strange the sense.

Yet, I do not hate the gun, nor the one firing.

I cannot condemn the hunter,
yet saw not the hunter in me.

MUSEO DELLA SINDONE

We came to Turin from Genoa to see this place, dedicated to a man
from Palestine who died on a cross—the
    Romans' singular (and horrible)
punishment for thieves, insurrectionists,
    and unwanted or dangerous
persons—wrapped in cloth in the Jewish fashion of the time.
Kept in an airtight glass and metal container
    in the Cathedral of Saint
John, tested, analyzed, peered at through an
    electron microscope, pored
over, studied by physicists, chemists, plant scientists, experts in the
making of cloth, and scoured for traces of dust, pollen, blood.

Scanned by x-ray tomography, strange image of a man scourged,
crucified, brutalized, blood puddled, weird
    photo-negative yielding an
eerie three-dimensional ghostlike image. Masterful forgery by some
medieval artist, or the real deal, for what technology centuries ago
could create such a thing?
But with faith, does it matter if such cloth
    covered the body of Christ,
or that of some medieval stone mason or
    watchman paid a few bits as model for
this strange creation, this icon of impossible belief?

Some believe a newborn babe may snatch
        the soul of one who has gone
before, or that a man may be reborn in animal form. Did Moses spy
a burning bush or hear the voice of God? For once a painter saw the
crucified Christ in the face of a dying Roma,
        crown of thorns, cudgels
that flailed his bleeding body.

Pollen samples, images of the cloth's intricate
        weave, spikes like those
said to have pierced Jesus' feet and wrists,
        recreation of the loom that
may have woven the cloth, of the chest in
        which the shroud was stored,
its survival miraculous after a fire in 1532 in
        Sainte-Chapelle in Chambéry.
Melting the silver container had burned holes
        in the precious fabric, this
bizarre obsession with relics, fleshy things,
        testament of the invisible.
But what does this prove? So, I conclude the shroud is a forgery,
a dazzling and masterful one. Unless it is not
        … but is in fact the burial cloth
of a Judean Jew, native tongue Aramaic.

And I would speak to Jesus myself, asking, "Who are you?"
Then ask the same of our master forger.

WORK

I was, of course, sent to buy coffee and breakfast for the crew,
descending then climbing the spiral metal stairs to the building's
roof, where I pulled up worn shingles, and carried tools and rolls
of tarpaper. The men on the crew joked about women and
stupid professors, one of whom was decapitated when a board
sticking out his car window was swiped by another vehicle
(they laughed). But I learned the meaning of labor on the roof of
Yale's Woolsey Hall, eighty feet above the ground, sidewalks
roped off to protect the public from death
     from above in the form of a
metal wrench, sander, or pail of cement.

Even today, I walk clear of these spaces, but
     then, working long and hard was
what I needed. For there is something beautiful
     in the doing and the making,
in labor connected to the hidden wants and
     needs of art, though not to
be romanticized or mythologized. Indra's
net, where all is interconnected as the Huayan patriarch
Dushun tells us: "Nothing comes or goes."
So, I think of myself as both causing and caused—what I was then,
and what I've done, become, and understood
     better with distance and time.

Mound and pyramid builders, stonemasons, carpenters,
bricklayers, builders, and fixers... Do not denigrate the
worker, or any worker, but neither glorify, for bone
and sinew means you are slave to the whimsies and
accidents of the human frame, in which mishap, slip, or fall
can end a career or bring death. Heavy rolls of tarpaper,

tearing up worn shingles, hammering, and carrying pails of
scraps are mixed with the recollection of a strange concert
in the hall itself by a man (a Yale music student?) banging
pots and pans, honking horns, clanging hubcaps, junk
and scraps of metal, clinking kitchen utensils, plastic
basins, makeshift cymbals, drums, clapboards, bottles, jugs,
and metal tubes, at which we laughed until tears flowed from
our eyes.

It seemed uncomplicated, that life in which I learned that
others work with their hands, the clang clang of the metal
spiral stairs, Memorial Rotunda in the Beaux Arts style,
images of the Nine Muses and the goddess Athena,
vestibule with plaques for Yale students who'd lost their
lives in American wars.

Thanatologos

For it is as if I am standing
on the precipice of a deep chasm,
opposing cliff in the distance
shrouded in mist.

And can barely be seen, shifting
changing, sometimes menacing
visage, an invented thing.

I knew little of death when I
was ten; then Uncle Izzy
died, smoker of cigars, inveterate
talker, diabetic.

Buried in a plain
pine coffin, distant as a squall
at sea.

Uncle Abe from a heart attack.
Aunt Mary, emphysema
from years in a hair salon.

Each death
a fiery smoking brand, or not,
for the sting comes slowly,
felt not in hopeful years.

Then one day an unwelcome
visitor comes, of iron mien,
but the sad truth is
I felt little.

As coffins lowered meant
only that someone old
enough to die had died.

And I had not.

The Island

Anticipation, loss, wonder, amazement, longing,
sadness, locked inside or dead.

Suffering that strange malady of museum goers,
we are infected with the irrefutable unreality of it:
the mystery of existence.

To have been born here, not there, now, not then.
Still, I must watch,
see,
know the riddle of past things that fade if we do not care.

A river of humanity passed through there,
each inch and foot sacred in a sense, a treasury
of memory, a yawning gap I can never know.

Each had another life, kept in a bottle or on a
shelf, and but for an accident of birth, I could be
one of them.

For sorrow rides close to the earth.

Shadows

A memory beneath an ocean. I about six years old,
Father doing what good fathers should do when
parents' loom large. The way of things. Vaguely, I
recall the observation deck of the Empire State
Building, his duty somehow to show me things
there, but I do not see him.

I remember not the car ride, nor entering the building,
nor the elevator ride to the top—or perhaps I do in
a dream, with intimate knowledge of sacred past happenings,
a symphony of loss even in the happiest recollection.
For it is about me, or some other self in the mists of
vanishing time ... about Father now gone.

But the view from atop the Empire State was
magnificent, confounded now with another view from
a tower disappeared in a column of fire. So, now it's
all a jumble of memories, habitually melding,
flattening, warping, and woofing things past into
a strange cauldron of colored recollection.

For I was of an age when little beyond the womb
of family could exist, a world where reports by a
neighbor of a suicide reached me with a strange
unreality, a lesson in what adults knew, curious
lucidity in a moving picture show, recollection,
perplexity at the passing of time.

The hazy city I recall, the lookout deck, the railing about
head height, then a step to stand upon to see the great urbe
sprawled, Hudson and East Rivers, Brooklyn and Upper

Bay, Chrysler Building and Central Park. But of course,
I knew none of these places, only vast space and the
horizon, Father there and not there, as am I.

Perhaps then to a diner for lunch, or a walk in Central
Park, salt pretzel (these I remember well!), an ice-cream
cone, or a look at horses and carriages on West 59th
Street, Father so reassuring and full of purpose mysteriously
drained from him in later years. Now he is gone, roots
and branches in evening's fading light.

Pilgrimage

There is a rhythmic flowing (Aristotle's *peripatetic*
in contact with the passing world) towards an unknown
yet desired goal.

The peeling of an onion, paring of excess to the essential.
But not all walking is the same, smoothing rough edges
of reality.

Changing, shifting of the as-yet-unknown quest,
myself and other than myself, without hinderances
or boundaries.

Without wanting, needing, craving, regret, sadness,
jealousy, hate, confusion, morality, or deception.
Where time, if it means anything at all, means nothing.

Solitude's winnowing chaff leaving only the durable
core in its untamed wildness, the necessary self's
discomfort, even pain, but pleasure also.

Then there was beauty in being alone, a cleansing
everywhere and nowhere, always the return with new
eyes, always the departure and return.

Past welcoming ports without setting anchor, peregrine
follower of the ancestors' way, knowing the journey ends
where it began.

THALASSA

I fear the sea, yet am drawn to it,
the blood of the earth; I feel its
depths even as I move from the shore,
its beauty, savageness, sublime in its moods.

So, it is true I have watched from the
high deck of a ship, waves crashing
in blackness, primal dread the stuff
of nightmares. But then, in morning
light, placid water as delicious green
as Murano glass gives the lie to
night terrors.

The sea has been so many things
to me: the soft, warm sand from
family outings; a lonesome, pebbly
beach on the island of Lesvos;
haunting promontory a hundred yards
from shore; rowing a red-painted dory
in Rockport harbor, age fifteen,
during the lost summer
of seventy-one.

And there are ocean worlds
spinning in the void of space I imagine
sailing, these too in some crazy black
dream. A modern Odysseus on wine-dark
seas, scion of landsmen in their
tombs. Or sitting on the deck of a
masted sloop, legs dangling, savoring
ocean-spray on my face and arms.

Wooden ships kissing the slow curve
of earth, tremulous wives and
daughters pacing Nantucket widow's
walks, joined in ecstasy and hurt to the
sea; Maine's craggy shore, Bar Harbor,
and Acadia's red-sand beach, flying
fish leaping due north in the golden
Philippine Sea, volcanic peaks rising
from coral banks.

These and more have been the sea to me.

TRACES

From the foreign land of memory, searching
for an apartment with Father one sultry oak-green
Connecticut August in 1975. To me, at all
of nineteen, he was friend, helper, confidant,
encourager, admonisher, storyteller, and
(I cannot forget) sometime bankroller, as I
inched towards adulthood, both wanting and
not wanting it.

Apartments we found none, though there was
one dank below-ground dungeon with two dirty
windows near the ceiling, suitable only for
for Dostoyevsky's Underground Man. So,
we moved on to a small Jewish cemetery
to find the grave of my great-grandfather
Abraham, born in Russia 1855, died in New
Haven in 1933. Father walked straight to
the grave he knew from childhood as I
stood by, yet strangely, I recall neither the
stone nor the words upon it, or if they were in
English or Hebrew.

About Abraham I know little, only that he
was Father's grandfather, carried across the sea
in his fifties, old by the thinking of those days.
What he must have left, I can hardly imagine,
childhood friends, synagogue, even parents.
How he earned his living, I cannot say, tailor,
scribe, merchant, lost now to relentless time.
Did he learn English, the language of his
adopted land, lost as well to memory and days?

There is sadness when I think of his untended
grave, like so many I have seen, Abraham,
son of Abraham, for the dead do not care,
though the living may for years; later my sister
and I came again, searching in vain for the
stone, memory serving only to say it was there,
a lonely stone in a sea of grass, gentle green
leafy boughs, and what is left after so many
years, nearly ninety to my count?

Tangled remnants of lives once lived, hopes
made to sleep, recollection drowned—
we looked, sister and I, hoping to hear him
call to us, but nothing, and I think of Father,
and I hovering between child and man, he
somehow understanding. When death had
not touched me as it does now, when only
those needing to die died.

Great-grandfather, more distant still, gone
twenty years before I was born. Do I have
his eyes, ears, mouth, hair? Obedient soldiers,
stationed there, belying unspoken history of
those below, a book—nay, many books—
dusty and never to be read. And now,
forty-seven years have passed, Mother and
Father gone, and I am alone, for the living
have their day, as do
the dead.

FROM A DISTANCE

A house with many doors,
infinite spiral staircase,
billowing clouds before a storm,
echo chamber of recall.

Secret etchings on a magic screen,
silent symphony of lost chords,
gateless gate,
marble statue in pouring rain.

Smoke wafting upwards,
a cool mountain stream,
placid recollections,
turbulent eddies in rushing waters.

Forgotten dreams,
serene embrace of distant fears,
passion recalled in tranquility,
tranquility recalled, passionately.

A bat winging,
an eagle soaring,
blind mole crawling,
endless mirrors.

Anguish of knowing,
joy of the moment,
the infinite,
dying and being reborn.

Visions of madness,
ecstasy of oblivion,
ancestors speaking from the grave,
magic lantern in an empty shed.

Everyone I've never met.

All the colors, beams of
woven thread,
the Skin
alight that
warms itself
with life[4]

RAMBLES

Bodyless, nearly invisible, no longer anyone
or anything,
to disappear for a time, forget myself in
the craggy bone-dry peaks
of the Sinai at sundown, spectacular almost beyond
description in the waning light
and shadow, like the surface of Mars,
such a place where it is said God spoke to Moses.
Not hard to imagine,
as if beauty could call forth the strange
and beyond human,
glowing mountains humming
in the pale evening,
crystal water of the sea, sunrise
over painted mountains.

Sights and sounds of Lomé, senses alive,
for everything spoke of the new,
pungent smack of open drainage canals in the
heat and humidity, dust and the faint
scent of the sea nearby,
deep, damp scent of tropical life,
pungent sweat though not unpleasant,
of lived life, cologne mixed with
orange and papaya, circle

of women chanting, rhythmic
syncopated beat.

The open road, thumb out,
mountains rising in the distance,
sailing down the Utah spine
in a Chevy pickup from Salt Lake to Provo,
Price and Moab, stark beautiful lands,
kissing the azure sky,
fast friends with a driver I will never see again.
Owning and loving the land, its
dusky browns and dark greens.

Then by the Nile, in the
sultry evening, ships pass by as if
a dream, millennia collapsed to
the present moment, palms lining the eternal
waterway, nameless and faceless I.
A place of the mind, not the body, dark water
carrying the watcher towards the sea,
earth pregnant with scattered atoms
of emperors and tradesmen,
farmers and stone carvers,
gentle breeze of forgetting, the *felah*
working the land, burnt by the sun,
turban wrapped about the head.
I gaze at the moving waters ripped
by wind.

Hours alone in silence, echo upon echo,
extending to the edge of the universe.
Thought and desire, fears, and intimations,
forked futures mirrored in
crystal lakes, placid waters, and forests
to discover oneself, or be lost forever,

timeless haunting as if humanity's
sojourn were but a cosmic blip,
funny and tragic. But come sunrise,
arrows through stands of pine,
earth's electric vibration
waking animals to the day's arrival,
dew
shimmering
as dregs of night are
miraculously cleansed.

Queenstown

This poem is about a visit to a place
on the South Island of New Zealand,
but really, it's about flowers … and also
about memory, what one remembers
and what one doesn't, mysterious
shadowy portals of recollection.

On a beautiful lake, mountains in the
distance, supermarket, restaurants,
passable sidewalks, a small park, all
tidy and clean, our tiny apartment
with a kitchenette, but it's the
flowering bush with a profusion
of pink and white blooms I recall
the best.

And so it struck me then,
as it does now, that beauty, in
nature (or maybe anywhere) cares
not for us, or anything perhaps, but
just is…

By a sidewalk, a wooden fence,
a road, an asphalt parking lot—there
was the bush (a bougainvillea, I
think), saying, *"I do not care …
for I am simply myself."*

A lesson in a way.

Mother's Day

It has been nearly three months since she
    died at ninety-eight,
and now that day comes, so yes, the obvious,
    she is simply gone
and cannot receive the greetings, she who
    gladly received them, always.

A well without water, the time of memory,
    sentiments and habits,
mythical and unreal, of nostalgia, recollected
    pasts waxing and waning with the
drifting, old memories like buoys, farther now,
    closer to the fearful, unavoidable
forgetting, the world of shades that terrifies me.

    What is left when someone dies?
Forget the body, for it is gone,
    or if not gone,
    meaningless,
or less than meaningless.
    And what was less real
becomes
    tangible in quiet hours.

She who stayed up late to help a fifth grader
    write a report on whales,
who served meatloaf and canned string beans
    for dinner, and worried when I left home at twenty
    for the highway and mountains.
Who believed in democracy, racial justice, the
    importance of honesty, and the

       sanctity of the vote.
Who had an eye for literature
       and art, though she couldn't attend
       college, and felt at home with Italians, though she was
       Jewish.
Who taught me Yiddish words,
       a thousand years old,
       and remembered the ice man,
       and movies for a quarter,
       the Depression, World War Two, and President
       Roosevelt.

There is a certain pleasure in remembrance,
though pain also.
The ideal
cannot replace the real
for memory serves up
       echoes, catching one's shadow
fleeing as we grasp.

Yet memory is what we have,
       there for us as time's
       ramble takes us on an autumn hayride,
       half wild, confident, then unsure
if I can make a picture that will quell the loss,
       knowing there will be no
more pieces than those I have.

But memory,
       thankfully,
is generous,
as I will know then
what I have not known.

Forest Walk

Dry earth blanketed with pine needles.
I see the trunks of great trees, brown and
rough and straight, and it is my soul too
hovering above and beside me.

Beyond easy words that call upon beauty
and sadness and awe, primeval if it can
be named, a doppelganger of myself
on the path of time.

Though unaware of it,
expansive and cosmic we must be,
for why do we live, struggle, and contend? Ecstatic
forgetting, strangely, to be no one.

Yet, there was always the return, the going-
from-here-to-there-and-back, by one who
thought of himself as immortal, aches not
calling forth the shadow of mortality.

Still, visits to tombs tell another story,
portents too, even from beloved nature,
things not heard in youth. Then somehow,
alas, the city walk replaced the forest walk.

Rivers

I return to waters as the emblem of my youth.
They were the cool interlude on a hot summer day,
wading barefoot with friends at thirteen,
because July meant no school, three months endless.

The river, which once powered mills, though free of
them now, stone foundations standing sentinel to
buildings long decayed. Slippery bottom of smooth,
round stones, eons old.

Walking shallow narrows under a lush, green canopy,
forming a tunnel, for the sheer fun of it,
looking for nothing, cool on feet and ankles, our river
because we had claimed it.

Sometimes raucous, muddy, and swollen, ominously
overflowing its banks, yet for us in summer
shallow and deliciously cool. River of hopes and
dreams, wonderment, and uncertainty.

Yet there were others, wider, roiling, splashing,
twisting, dancing, swirling. Slippery boulders
carried from northlands by towering glaciers, icy
waters winding through verdant pines, gnarly oaks.

At home under wooden bridges, loamy bends—
into these waters I did not wade but rather sat
on shore, watching foamy whitecaps everchanging,
curling, exploding, only to be replaced instantly.

Heraclitus' moving waters of my youth, shadows
flitting amid faint voices, words and faces faded
though still present in the spaces between trees,
splashing water's sonorous music.

Water fresh as *yin* and *yang*, pine-scented dirt
so fine, I would sit for an hour watching and
watching, the river speaking, anchored in time—
a dreamtime of yearning.

This river where I once quietly fished in the
shade of a covered bridge, where I forged myself
unknowing, secret longings unfulfilled,
intimations of beauty, sacredness.

Sinews more than intellect, still though searching,
flitting dappled sunbeams on the cool, clear water
where canoes paddled familiar eddies, peaceful
in their time.

Farther south were rivers slow flowing, rust dark,
narrow, looping, out of some vernal prehistoric
picture, sun barely reaching mirror waters, joyful
abandon through forests of low-hanging bows.

Verdant growth, days and nights gone forever in
the furnace of advancing years, memory's absent
worry in the fleeting afternoon of youth. Then, still
deeper, flow waters through steamy jungles.

Where caiman poke heads into air, gleaming
slanted eyes, wiry monkeys make jungle-gyms
of overhung branches, howler calls echoing.
Thus descend our souls.

Merging with what has passed, for we are children
of forgotten lineages tangled like wild vines—and
in the shadow of wanderings, we sit by dancing
fate, casting life adrift.

THAT WAS THEN

First grade in Horace Mann school,
Columbia University,
Father busy getting his doctorate.
Memories somehow both vague and clear:
Miss O'Connor, my teacher,
a young black woman
whose kind face I recall,
her endless patience
with six-year-olds—
in her nineties now, if she
lives still—but it was the kangaroo rats
I remember best
for she had set up a large plywood box
with a wire-mesh top,
full of fine sand, rocks, and
small plants mimicking the creatures'
desert home.
So, we were taught
to care for these small hopping animals,
care entrusted to six-year-olds,
a lesson I understood not then,
though more so now, and am thankful for,
unknown to we children:
lessons in caring, even loving,
respecting living things,
watching them eat as we fed them
sunflower seeds, their digging and
scratching, darting about, sleeping,
sniffing, an act of courage (I now realize)
for what if one died?
How to explain this to children?

And I remember peering
into the box, watching them hop about.
At the age of six, what do we know?
Yet still such things change us, seedlike,
making us the persons we are
meant to be. To understand
what it means to be alive, no less,
to cherish life itself.
Then there was Miss O'Connor, laughing heartily
when I told her, standing in the coatroom
amid dutifully hung winter jackets,
unsightly red blotches on my face,
that she should not worry,
for "it's just the German measles."
In this small world, all was done
for me. Miss O'Connor, with her kind
smile and inviting laugh…
Might she remember me still?

In this cloistered world, I
knew nothing of John Glen,
Marilyn Monroe, rioting in
Mississippi, the Dow Jones,
the cost of gas or eggs per dozen,
the Bay of Pigs, DEFCON 2,
Nikita Khrushchev, ICBMs,
Bob Dylan, the price of a farm
in Wisconsin, Andy Warhol,
Chubby Checker, or many other things.
Sixty years has passed, and so,
another sixty I shall not have—
memories are lampposts:
Mother is sick in bed with the flu. It is my
first memory of her. She cannot rise.

A neighbor lady cares for me,
and my brother and sisters, for a few days,
as I obsessively repeat the lines
of a song I've heard. For I am
again in these places, having
lost something precious
I cannot name.

Dreams

At fourteen, I coveted a pair of brown leather zip-up boots
as I gazed through a plate-glass shop window,
across the expanse of the golf course I had to cross.
Object of desire, strange as I see them, projection
of wants and needs of growing up, too slowly
at times, dreams vague though they be, inchoate cast towards
uncertainty.

In truth, there seemed something magical about them.
Do they anchor us, separate us from the soil,
make us stronger, taller, fill us with confidence? Yet some
say we are better when we wear nothing, bare heels
hugging earth, electric current deep underground,
through peaks and steamy jungles.

Yet how I longed for those sleek leather boots behind the
plate glass (the shop long gone now, a supermarket
in its place), promising things I craved,
school a bother and distraction when what mattered was
roaming, to fill mornings and afternoons, whole days ...
irresponsibility a calling card and badge of honor.

At fourteen, I knew not much—I bought those leather boots with
money saved, drip drop, delivering papers in rain
and snow for those I admired yet secretly disdained,
rushing hurriedly to mature.

Thrown away long ago, these handsome boots are gone,
soles worn, uppers scuffed and scratched though
shined and waterproofed lovingly for several years—yet
strangely, I remember not the hour nor day these boots

were flung away in the whirl of years, things given or
lost. Where is the sled I pulled a hundred times to the hill
where we careened, my toboggan, my ten speed, the tobacco pipe
I coddled at fifteen as we roamed ... the musty sweet scent of
baseball glove, roller skates, skateboard, backpack, and
dented camp stove?

Just things, you say?
Perhaps. Yet in the flux felt only by the
young, somehow as the years have passed, the crisp
novelty, thick and dense as it was, half recalled, is still new,
emerging, deep, fluid, and wide, penetrating as if through
touch I could prove I was real.

For a day and a half, shoes made the boy, an age of "not quites,"
almost a man yet not, vague intimations on the cusp of
knowing. Then soon I traded smooth leather for mountain and
forest studs, coarse leather uppers and rough rubber soles,
leaving sleekness for others to perfect, closer to earth, where
we'll someday be.

In Praise of Forgetting

Bliss it is to forget for a moment,
or an hour, or a week,
to not be anything.

To forget I have a name,
to feel as cold, clear water at the
bottom of a well.

In praise of forgetting, this world
of troubles, of pain, of hurt, injustice,
and suffering known and unknown.

That the sky is blue, and the sea green.
That Lincoln was shot at Ford's
Theatre on April 14, 1865.

That my ancestors from Lithuania
were killed in the wave of madness
we call the Holocaust.

That I have a body and was born.
That I, like everyone else,
will die.

That I'll never be all I wish to be.
My separateness from forests, mountains,
and oceans.

In praise of forgetting that I could have
been a better man ... sometimes *was*
a better man.

That my parents have died.
That I am no longer young.
That the innocence
of childhood will never come again.

Un-Becoming

Just one of those small pleasures, a newly
       cleaned hotel room, pillows soft, sheets
       drawn tightly over the mattress.

Yes, it's self-indulgent and small, I know, yet
       a pleasure, nevertheless, for a brief few
       moments hiding like an ostrich in the glow
       of a bedside lamp, inspecting someone else's
       choice of wall hangings and furniture.

After a day dragging suitcases, dodging throngs,
       and squinting at plane, train, and bus tickets,
       delicious sliding from public to private.

But there's something else, hard to explain—
       I imagine myself as another (not anyone I
       know) for a moment, shutting out the world,
       my virtual self
       real for a fleeting slice of time.

Getting It

Some say growing old is the beginning of wisdom,
        and I say yes, but
the past seems that of another.
        Or to be more precise, happenings, places, and people
not different than those of Alexandria or Pompeii—
        a peculiar revelation. I know not why.
Some say too it is the body that grows old and not
        the mind.
And I say yes, but it is the body that must obey the
        the iron law of time.

Yet does the mind tire of the agony and joy of waking,
        of the metronome where laughter was once heard,
of walking in vertiginous paneled mansions where
        shadows reside?
What, then, of the years passing? Ordered and stacked
        as I am their owner, author, observer, warden, tamer,
lover, hater, judge, jury, gatekeeper, teller, killer,
        and devourer of shadows.

THE WORLD IS NEW

I would wake early Saturday morning, and tiptoe
downstairs at six a.m. to watch cartoons for an
hour before Mother rose to make breakfast. Solitude
at the age of eight. *Bugs Bunny*, *Wile Coyote*,
Rocky and Bullwinkle, *The Jetsons*, *The Flintstones*,
Popeye, *Magilla Gorilla*, *Underdog*, *The Pink Panther*,
Scooby-Doo... How I savored this time alone! So
silly these shows seem now, yet I loved them, and the
morning quiet, cross-legged on the floor, gazing
at our small black and white TV. It was *The Jetsons*
that truly captivated me though, with its airy, optimistic vibe.

Mother would rise at seven to make breakfast, French
toast or pancakes, and then I (not allowed coffee,
though I was a good eater) would leave the table with a
full stomach and a nod. But those cartoons stayed with me,
lessons in storytelling though I knew it not, silly
as they were.

My hermetic life, not quite Edenic,
though happy enough, too young to know or care
about the world that raged and trembled, for in
1964, the Olympic flame was lit by a man born in
Hiroshima the day an atomic bomb destroyed the
city; a black man was blasted with a fire hose during
a riot in Rochester; Beatlemania swept through the
Unites States; Fidel Castro pitched nine innings;
Bob Dylan jammed; 500-pound bombs pulverized
the Viet Cong; an earthquake struck Alaska; Muhammad
Ali met Malcolm X; fifty were slaughtered in Zambia; East

Germans escaped through a tunnel; and Norman
Rockwell met astronauts.

All this I knew not,
partaking the blissful emptiness of a container
eager to be filled, not yet weary, nor thinking it
would be a curse to live for a thousand years, or yet
buried under the detritus of winter upon winter,
the child holding the lantern.

Those quiet moments
strange and precious now, a curious
hovering, wants and needs in abeyance, memory
now the bubbly broth of desire—so I return to my
favorite cartoon, depicting an (almost) perfect future,
where the balm of technology solves all problems
while behemoth Armageddon hovers.

But to an eight-year-old,
the narcotic siren call of future life,
fever-dream Sputnik and techno-spawned robotic Astro,
seemed sweet indeed, nature banished save for the
green splash of an occasional potted plant.
All gone.

Those sweet mornings in winter when,
upon waking, fresh snow glistened
as I gazed out frosted windows,
meaning school had been cancelled.
So, I would bundle up in snow boots, gloves,
long johns, knitted cap, two pairs of
socks, and a scarf to romp in the
powdery white.

And when temperatures
dropped while wind howled,
it was
sweeter still,
the delectable sting on my cheeks
welcome.

Oh, how I wish my life were an ox-cart
That rolls along squeaking in the early morning
Going back later to where it came from
By the same road as night falls!

FERNANDO PESSOA[5]

ODE TO PLACES I'VE NEVER BEEN

Mountains capped with snow, straight pines, a cabin
small of knotty cedar, hearth of handsome stone, fire
burning bright, casting dancing shadows on the wall.

A great rock set by glaciers strong, where people
of the west wind rest in the cool shade of midday.

Before roaring crystal waters, voracious under azure
sky, cataracts glint in the aluminum sun.
Only the eagle sees.

A bar in Île de la Cité where a man in a red vest
and a woman with braids sit quietly drinking coffee.
It is late afternoon and fanciful clouds cast
playful shadows on the Seine.

The serene spot on the River Ouse where Virginia Woolf
drowned herself. The last bit of dry land she touched.

The island of Paros, where Archilochus was born. The
shaded grove where he wrote, *"Let us hide the Sea-King's
gifts, the wrecked dead Poseidon brings."*

The bottom of the ebony sea, where the coelacanth

glides unseen, neither knowing nor caring for
the world above.

Mumbai's Zoroastrian Towers of Silence, where the
dead are devoured by vultures.

Potala Palace, with its thousand rooms, dizzying mandalas,
prayer wheels, guardian spirits, sonorous bells,
myriad hues, and ten thousand shrines. The Tengyur
Sutra I shall never see nor read.

Čachtice Castle, bastion of the Blood Countess. Zaire's Ituri
rainforest, mother and father of the Mbuti people.

Buenos Aires' Recoleta Cemetery, City of the Dead and
the tango, where Eva Perón, Domingo Sarmiento, and
Facundo Quiroga are buried.

Its tombs and alleys, forlorn inscriptions, doves and stone
crosses, bronze statue of Liliana Crociate and her dog Sabú,
Rufina Cambaceres, who died twice.

The cities of Umma and Badtibira, where lesser gods bow
before Inanna. Inanna where she lives still, the luxuriant.

That secret place where lovers meet in the shade of the old
oak. The soft mossy ground they lay on, their initials
carved on the massive trunk.

Lake Colden in January

Bathed in white

that could have meant beauty, the sublime,

serenity, or death.

I was twenty, hearty of frame, free of the

vexing worries of the flesh.

We young and careless ones,

abandoned to the eternal moment,

so unlike the years gathered

like a funnel of time and loss.

Vanished Things

Mother's smile
Wheelies on my red stingray
Delivering the *New Haven Register* on a cold February morning
Hopping the fence at dusk to a deserted expanse of green
Dewy grass as I walked by starlight
Feeling part of a protected world
Inventing language as air breathed
At peace with not knowing
Father's calming advice
Embrace of forest
Crunch of pine needles
Whiff of earth after hard rain
Scintillated sky at night
Sweet scent of oiled baseball glove
Sharp crack of bat on ball
Boundless energy at thirteen
Lying on cool grass watching fireworks
Campfire shadows on darkened forest
Splashing in mountain streams
Sound of the sun rising
Crickets in early evening
Catching fireflies
Father's Ford station wagon
Camping the Housatonic
The rush of the river
Fishing Bulls Bridge in Kent
Pleasant fragrance of aged wood
Child who died at birth
Legs aching from miles walked

Biking the hills of Cape Breton
Father teaching me to write a check
Shaving for the first time
Fearing to enter a Catholic church
Learning Hebrew for my Bar Mitzvah
Passover with Uncle Leon and Aunt Lillian
Johnny Carson, the Vietnam War, Lyndon Johnson
Bobby Kennedy, Martin Luther King
Magruder film and grassy knoll
Sirhan Sirhan, Mom's pot roast
Asking for a date and being turned down
Smoking hash for the first time
Wrestling brother (almost) to the death
Smoking hash for the second time
Evenings under neighborhood streetlight
Sunrise in Newfoundland
Waves crashing in Lomé
Breaking windows at age ten
Getting caught
Waiting for Armageddon's crimson glow
Learning to swim
The Muppets, John Denver, Secretariat, Betamax,
floppy disks, Nixon, pet rocks, shag carpets, water beds,
Frank Zappa...
Sleeping under the stars
Falling in love on the New York subway
Seeing death
Lunch below the Acropolis
Lotus in a Japanese zendo
Sonorous Muslim call to prayer
Father's wisdom
Mother's love

Stealing from a supermarket at ten
Getting caught
Salted pretzel with Father
Manhattan in '63
Hypnotic beat of African drums
All these things I knew.

Nishi Hongan-ji

If there is peace, it is on the cool wooden floor of a

                  Buddhist hall.

Founder Shinran's dream, disciple of Hōnen's Pure Land.

I will never be a good Buddhist for I am too much

                  the doubter,

yet Pure Land, so simple in a way: enlightenment

through verse, chanting a special phrase,
    expressing gratitude to Amitābha,

his boundless compassion.

It is a beautiful thought, not irrelevant to our present time,

balm to our new age of *mappō*, mentioned centuries ago by Huisi.

The Final Dharma, a great foreboding. Still, the *Nihon ryoiki* asks,

            "How can we live without doing good?"

        Compassion, the bottomless gift, the Primal Vow,

for the dispossessed, the poor, *samsāra* exploded to deliver the self,

      through renunciation of self-effort, letting
      go, through simple faith

in utterance of the Name, the working of the Vow.

I am awed as I wordlessly sit.

For a moment, I believe, feel the beauty,

the power of it, glimpse the depth of mind and spirit.

As if the world implodes into itself.

How pitiful that the spring winds of
impermanence should so abruptly
scatter the beauty of the blossoms.

The Tale of the Heiki[6]

What enormous pleasure
In time of youth, when hope has such
            great distance
To travel still and memory so little.

Giacomo Leopardi[7]

The Big One

We of the sixties and seventies grew up with it,
ate and drank it, absorbed it by osmosis. We lived it
yet never loved it, this rot at the heart of everything,
a dead thing we slept and cuddled with. Kennedy,
Khrushchev, and the Cuban Missile Crisis, seeping into
us, though we knew it not, our *danse macabre.*

A strange and singular memory: nuclear-attack
drills in fourth grade, classroom coatroom, where we
were told to huddle down, heads between our legs in
preparation for ... what? A blinding flash, a blast of
superheated air, incineration, or perhaps the collapse
of the building itself? All done in immaculate calm
by Miss Ginzburg, so as not to alarm we young ones.

I banged my funny bone, forearm numb and throbbing,
a moment of panic, and then it was over, back to our seats, to
lessons, recess. Our peculiar weekly ritual so little
understood (thankfully) by seven-year-olds. I thought
nothing of it.

Yet something must have stuck, sunk in, grabbed
hold, a creeping, slinking awareness that the world is a dangerous,
unpredictable place, where death can come at any
moment, mixed smoothly with the quotidian, the
the regular and expected, even hoped for and loved—
the weird *zeitgeist* of those funny times.

How could we have known? Built in 1910, grand Mayflower
School had seen the Great War, Franklin Roosevelt, Charlie
Chaplin, and many other things, yet we saw mostly what
they wanted us to see, except when we didn't. The Beatles,
Ed Sullivan, Elvis Presley, jigsaw of excitement and unease,
a pregnant churning of change belied by the calm of our elders.

Then strangely, at twenty-five, the fear hit me, visceral, haunting,
and tangible, dread like I'd never known bubbling up ...
dread of non-existence, ceasing to be, losing everything,
not having time to put things in order,
of missing out, being blotted out, of joining the vast mute
dead, the unknown, being alone, not having been loved enough,
not having loved enough, seen enough, done enough.

Yet, eventually, these things passed, as did the intimation of
Armageddon's crimson glow, the laughter, and dread too, though
what replaced it was less life. These were strange times on the
cusp of the Age of Aquarius, for I now
          know even less about the cost
of death, that blank white sheet. Still, the world goes on,
a child beyond understanding.

And so, my return to the necessary land of ignorance ... for what
good would knowing have done when crossing the street safely
and learning the names of states were of more importance?
Finally, though, the awakening came, unwelcome as it was.

Or, perhaps, it happened in dribs and drabs,
the worries of my elders seeping slowly
into my brain,
like a man leaping from a burning building.

Last Stop

It was time,
    that dreaded calling,
louder as the years passed,
        yet always the thought: *It's not here.*
Then it came finally, that unpleasant day
when children become parents, strange
    brew of shame, pain, hope,
sadness, and resignation, denial's narcotic.
        So, there we were, excitement feigned,
touring dining hall,
    exercise room, auditorium,
        computers, and billiard room,
somnolent corridors amid
muffled shuffling, bookcases, and flowers,
    framed pastel pictures
        that in some way I liked
            and was terrified by,
while we sons and
    daughters observed with opaque
detachment
    through blue-tinted glass, the neighbor,
    who bent as a crooked stick, died
    like clockwork.
Lunch and dinner, however, were pleasing,
        "like a restaurant almost,"
strawberry shortcake
(my favorite) while seated,
    hermetic cliques wavering astern,
        hovering queerly
as we breathed
        the unreal.

I recall the swarm of details, the texture of
        carpets, the antiseptic smell, the politeness of
            some and blank expressions of others,
                handsome young servers, halls
you could get lost in, tidy frames,
diminutive café, mail cubbies,
        but alas,
            it wasn't home,
and we knew it—could feel it deep down.
    A thought to be stuffed into an airtight locker,
tied to a rock,
            and cast into the sea.
                We knew.

GRIEF

They stay just out of reach,
despite my calling and calling,
that eerie sensation
of leaden feet in a dream,
tearless and voiceless,
in flames of regret.

Months pass, then years,
while those we love
fade frighteningly from memory,
as if some inexorable
    force pulls from
      a distance,
        an entropy of the soul,
           wrenching us apart
                atom
                   by
                     atom.

MUSIC

I am no musician
though sometimes in my dreams
    I imagine
playing the blues on a seven-stringed guitar, or
swaying to the beat of rhythmic
    African drums syncopated to
        the thrum of my heartbeat,
          driving, thumping
      walls of sound.
Though music was never in the cards for me,
it is in my blood,
      chords that blow off
      the top of my head,
    electricity in my veins,
jolt scorching the moment,
causing me
      to lose myself in ecstasy,
    my link to the ancient ones,
before computers, watches, cars, gunpowder,
iron, steel, bronze, dams,
        even the wheel.
How sound confers power to melt upwards,
    kick away
ropes that bind,
sweet secret key found a thousand generations past,
    bringing a stick to the beat
      of a heart
when another joined.

Old Friends

I have reached that age when
there is more looking back
than forward,

a consolation and a source of sadness,

hackneyed, though deep and true,
because all are subject to the iron grip,
majestic and terrifying.

I see them as they were at sixteen and twenty,

strong of arm and clear of eye, in the
sureness of knowing there is a future,
beautiful, though we did not see it then.

With hearts of wind, days seemed

long enough to fit dreams given wings,
if only for an hour until the sinking of
the sun, like princes to rise again.

Death then had no quarter, no sting,

for I was ten before I saw the yawn
of an open grave.

Locus Amoenus

There always seemed another world, just out of reach, that I could
almost touch, only to see it vanish, miragelike, hovering in the
hinterlands of my mind. Vague sentiment, hard to put into words,
and so, in my own modest way, I have been a searcher for a time
in boreal forests, where I disappeared for weeks at a time, trees,
streams, and windswept peaks my dear friends and solace,
embracing silence in the amber green and loamy earth.

Years later, this solitude is a marvel and mystery to me, for I
craved the sound of wind in valleys and leeward slopes, braver
then, more determined perhaps than the fear that hangs like
a curtain over things. Pain I once pursued less welcome now as it
comes uninvited and in stranger ways. Yet still there was
something sweet—child and sire of nostalgia—tempered by the
hour glass's wavering shadow.

Then it was water, roiling, cleansing, turbulent, and clear,
emblem of change, faith, mirror of my unformed self, water
so cold it would take my breath away, leave me for a moment
stunned. And it is water I again long for now, absolver of
    more protean
cares. Yet still that sublime space remains, once seen and always
there, a primal repose after long toil and a return to simpler things,
some gone the darkling way.

Broad open lands, promising long life and artful forgetting,
gentle breezes, seagulls wheeling on halcyon tides, the incessant
pull of opaque desire. No more the fierce burnings, steep
ascents, nor icy plunges, yet still there is that other world,
clearer though distant still, real as it ever was, in a dream,
waters of my youth, meadows kissed by warming sun.

Make an island for yourself. Hasten
and strive.

The Dhammapada[8]

The Roar of Silence

I have sat at the feet of teachers, who have sat at the
feet of masters, so I have touched enlightenment
thrice removed, which has the feeling of a handsome
baseball glove in a shop window that I have
not the money to buy.
I know this feeling well, yet still live
in the hope of that clap of thunder, which is sudden
illumination. Still, truth be told, I am patient now
that the years have passed, heeding advice that beauty
is in the here and now, before us always. Sweet it is
to sit in early morning quiet in the wooden zendo
with its fresh scent as the sun rises in the forest, in
the simplicity of this act, doing nothing, save following
the body's rhythmic breath, as earth exhales in a
moment of serene calm.

Not wanting, craving,
harming, grasping, pushing, or pulling.
A great cyclone
whirling, drifting strangely to the east, alive with
inexplicable energy, dawn breaks as it has for
eons, here in the presence of souls tethered to bodies
in the vastness of time, riding a cosmic wave. Cumulus
clouds mingle with the leafy forest canopy, and for
a few moments, troubles melt into nothingness, which
lies at the root, buzzing and crackling, a river in a
raging storm ... in the eye of which we sit.

There is a stove burning wood (for it is late November),
warmth bathing us, cold striking our faces when we leave
the hall, the shiny, polished floor, soft pillows, an
altar with flowers, a low bench, a small bell, an image
of the Buddha, sleek paneled walls, and low vaulted
ceiling. We are adrift in the deep of space. A bell
has rung, in ever-softening pulses, as thick silence
blankets us.

The trick is to find peace in this wild
world, topping mountains, all the while anchored
to earth; our teacher speaks of death, tells jokes and
stories: a Japanese monk buried under a keg of beer,
a sleepy disciple meditating on the rim of a well,
a hospice patient too proud to ask for help, a man
joyful on death's bed.

We sit on the floor and share as dusk
falls, shadows lengthening in the glow of evening's
lanterns, sonorous clang of bell setting calm air
vibrating. Beautiful it is. One has a story of addiction,
another a child's death. Then silence. A young woman
tells of peace as she lay awaiting an operation for
a brain tumor: "I knew all would be well."

Another cries, recalling her dog, stung to death by bees.
Silence again, as wind whistles in the cold evening air, the
hall a cocoon, balm, respite, splash of the real. We
are told of cycles, the timeless dharma. We complain
about politics, the slow pace of change, human
nature, violence, and suffering. We are told again of
cycles, the dharma.

Snow falls as the evening
puts on a cloak of white, recalling for me my

childhood as I gazed out at ivory drifts, only the
rhythmic breath now, in and out, mirroring
the hum of the cosmos, planets in their symphonic
revolution, our galaxy wheeling like the great
cyclone in my mind's eye, a projection
of this strange dream.

Now I Know

I knew no more, nor should I have,
yet somewhere in the years between then and now,
I began to understand.

First, Izzy died—Father's uncle on his mother's side.

Into a simple pine box he went, but this touched me not, for
it was not me. Then another died, and at a wake was laid,
as I marveled at the undertaker's art.

But it was not me. Others followed—Aunt Mary and
Uncle Abe—but still they were not me, and they
were old.

For when I was ten, a grave was just a hole in the ground.
But there is a voice, in search of a cocked ear, stranger,
lover, seducer, Janus, or friend.

Yet who will listen save the setting sun, and
where is the wisdom of age, so stealthily hidden?

THE SWIMMING

The place shines in my mind—water dripping
    cool from my body, for later-in-life ills of
    the frame held no fear in youth.
Bracing shock of splash on face, warmth of humid
August breeze, air caressing arms, legs, and chest.
    These are the imaginings of one who will live
    such in the mind, only now, to be young again:
a dream of fools. To have lived, that is all. Memories
fluttering and winking from some distant land,
    picture show on a wavering screen, exquisite,
        fleeting, sublime; again, birdsong in broadleaf
    tree, enticing, delicious burble of water, the
        momentary bob, then breath, future full of
mystery and desire, fugitive of passing years.

Palette of Scents

Spray of mist on dark-green seaweed-covered rocks.
    Waft of aged pine upon cracking the door of a cabin.

Crisp slap of Adirondack air, January, on a snowbound
    mountain trail.

Deep, rich loam of New England forest after a heavy rain;
    Mother frying bacon on a lazy Saturday morning.

Gentle breeze over the Nile at dusk, amid swaying palms;
    sweet, fresh puff of new-fallen snow at dawn.

Cigarette smoke on the platform in New Haven Union Station;
    musty drift of winter jackets in Grand Central.

Pungent smack of an open drain in Lomé; overripe bananas,
    sickly sweet, on my kitchen countertop.

Stench of armpit on a rush-hour bus; dewy grass at dawn
    on a vast expanse.

Pine-scented retsina in a bar in Nafplio; brochettes grilling
    over glowing coals in Sokodé.

Whiff of hashish as I wander Istanbul; a cornfield in
    Iowa as the sun rises.

Pancakes on a Sunday morning; strange metallic smell of blood.
    My down sleeping bag on a cold winter night.

Eggs frying on a camp stove; wisps of spray from a grotto's
     waterfall.

A freshly bought book, its newly printed pages; sultry summer
     evening with the boys in August of 1970.

Hay in a Canadian boxcar I once slept in; smoke from a
     campfire's dying embers.

Incense wafting upward in a Hindu temple; a dog's wet fur.
     The skin of a woman slept with.

Cannabis from the tip of a glowing joint; sweat, iron, and
     liniment in the weightroom of the New Haven YMCA.

Ripe durian fruit, a hot bowl of chili, fresh-baked bread,
     and sampaguita
     on the fence in my yard.

The chimp enclosure at the Bronx Zoo; every outhouse I ever
     visited. A mountain stream.

Skunk cabbage of my youth; my baseball glove, long since lost.
     Pine needles. Chicken soup. Mom's meatloaf.

Uncle Izzy's cigars and seldom swept apartment. Cast-
     iron oil-burning
     stove; the Costa Rican rainforest, Guanacaste.

Washed hair, feta cheese, a woolen blanket, cotton candy.
     Grilled sardines in Lisbon.

Moldy cheese, laundromats, the lumber warehouse where I worked.
     Cologne from ten feet away.

Ten thousand cattle, freshly brewed coffee, my pillow, cedar mulch.
Chocolate cookies just out of the oven.

Lavender soap, the milking stall at Cornwall farm in 1980, diesel,
and fast food at a truck stop.

Chamomile tea, basil, figs on the island of Crete. Phantom scents
that appear and disappear.

Mom's pot roast I never again shall eat.

L'Eau d'Issey, Acqua di Gio, cardamom, cinnamon, sandalwood,
vetiver, eucalyptus, frankincense, bergamot, wintergreen.

Benzoin, helichrysum.

The scent of youth, old age, fortune, and misfortune,
forgotten memory.

Of time passed…

Land of the Shades

For they sink slowly into a shadowy, forbidden world,
though likely they know it not, only we are left,
hands outstretched in supplication.

Wanting to touch what can no longer be touched,
what remains of those without whom I
could not have been.

Reduced they are to mementos and trinkets,
neatly placed on shelves, and photographs that have become
strange as the years pass.

It is a loss like no other when they shuffle off,
one for which I am unprepared and have no words,
a piece of childhood uprooted and cast adrift.

ENDNOTES

1   *Grave Matters*. From "Elizabeth Wood," ed. E.R. Shushan, (New York: Ballantine Books, 1990), 28.

2   "In the Garden of Time and Destiny," Part VI, sec, 6 "The Ottoman Empire and the Balkins," in *World Poetry: An Anthology of Verse from Antiquity to Our Time*, trans. Walter Andrews, Mehmet Kalpakli, and Najaat Black, ed. Katharine Washburn and John S. Major (New York: Norton, 1998), 668.

3   La Nature est un temple où de vivants piliers/Laissent parfois sortir de confuses paroles;/L'homme y passe à travers des forêts de symbols/ Qui l'observent avec des regards familiars (My translation).

4   From Akhenaton's "Hymn to the Sun" [c. 1375 B.C.E.], in *World Poetry: An Anthology of Verse from Antiquity to Our Time*, trans. John Pearlman, eds. Katherine Washburn and John S. Major (New York: Norton, 1998), 19.

5   Quem me dera que a minha vida fosse um carro de bois/Que vem a chiar, manhãzinha cedo, pela estrada/E que para de onde veio volta depois/Quase à noitinha pela mesma estrada. From "Alberto Caeiro" XVI. *Selected Poems of Fernando Pessoa*. University of Texas Press, 1971. p. 124 (My translation).

6   *The Tales of the Heiki*. Translated by Burton Watson. (New York: Columbia University Press, 2006), 143.

7   From "To the Moon". *The Canti with a selection of his prose*. Translated by J.G. Nichols. (New York: Routledge, 2003), 58.

8   Juan Mascaró. Trans. and Introduction (New York: Penguin, 1973), 70.

www.ingramcontent.com/pod-product-compliance
Lightning Source LLC
Chambersburg PA
CBHW032254070726
47590CB00016B/2802